Autism in Teens

By

Cindy Stringer Wismer

Pearls Publishing House

PPH

ISBN-13:978-1500291303

ISBN-10:1500291307

Dedicated to my forever friend, Nancy.

Table of Contents

Preface:

Parenting and/or teaching a teenager with autism requires a wealth of knowledge and understanding. After teaching for thirty-five years, mostly in the field of special education, I wish to share some of my acquired knowledge with you. My hope is that this book will help to make your journey a little smoother.

While I have used my best efforts in preparing this book, I make no warranties with the respect to the accuracy or completeness of the contents. The advice and strategies contained herein may not be suitable for your situation. You should consult with a professional where appropriate.

I would like to thank my friend, Nancy Daniel, for her ongoing support and encouragement; my niece, Maya, for allowing me to be a part of her world and giving me insight; and my husband Michael, for believing in me.

Autism is a disorder of neural development. Impaired social skills and interactions, and impaired communication are common characteristics. The autism spectrum (ASD) encompasses three disorders; autism, Asperger's Syndrome, and pervasive developmental disorder not otherwise specified (PDD-NOS).

The American Psychiatric Association's Diagnostic and Statistical Manuel, fifth edition (DSM-5) lists the following criteria:

-Persistent deficits in social communication and social interaction across multiple contexts- e.g., multiple contexts would refer to various settings; the deficits are apparent at school, home, and social situations.

-Deficits in social-emotional reciprocity- e.g., not able to carry on a back-and-forth conversation, reduction of shared interests with peers, fails to initiate or respond to social interactions

-Deficits in nonverbal communicative behaviors; e.g., poor eye contact, abnormal body language, inability to pick up on social cues from others

-Deficits in developing, maintaining, and understanding relationships

-Restricted, repetitive patterns, interests, or activities; e.g., repetitive motor movements, echolalia, lining up objects

-Insistence on sameness, inflexible adherence to routine; e.g., distress at small changes, rigid thinking patterns, greeting rituals, the need to take same the route or eat same food every day

-Highly restricted, fixated interests that are abnormal in intensity or focus

-Hyper- or Hypo- reactivity to sensory input or unusual interest in sensory aspects of the environment; e.g., adverse response to textures, sounds; excessive smelling or touching of objects; fascination with lights, vacuums, fans, etc.

To rephrase- A teenager with autism may have difficulty having a back-and-forth conversation with a friend. The teen with autism isn't really listening as his friend speaks, instead s/he is planning what s/he will say next. The conversation is one-sided with the teen with autism responding with information about her/his interest. Many teens with autism have fixated and perseverative interests. Some interests that I have seen in my classroom are; dinosaurs, Pokémon, video games, flags, volcanoes, wars, even the letter Q. Some children are so fixated on a movie they will literally memorize every line. The teen with autism finds it difficult to take turns and tends to monopolize the conversation.

A teenager with autism finds it difficult to understand the social cues. S/he may not be able to tell from another's facial expression or tone of voice how they are feeling.

Teenagers with autism may still have some of the repetitive behaviors from their childhood; pacing, flicking hands, rocking, repeating phrases or movie lines. Echolalia refers to a teen repeating what was said to them. For example, you might say, "Harry, would you like a hamburger?" and Harry's response may be, "Harry, would you like a hamburger?" or a shortened, "like a hamburger.

Causes and Demographics:

Autism is found in all racial, ethnic and socio-economic groups. Science does not know all the causes of autism. It is believed that some of the causes are environmental, biologic and genetic. Older parents have an increased risk. Siblings of children with autism are also at an increased risk. According to the CDC boys are four times more likely than girls to have ASD.

The Autism Spectrum

There are three major types of autism in the spectrum;

*Autistic Disorder- This is classic autism. The individual meets the criteria for poor social skills, poor communication skills, and repetitive behaviors.

*Asperger Syndrome- This is a milder form of autism without a language deficit. In fact, people with

Asperger's are often gifted. They do have limited interests, are socially awkward, and may talk non-stop about their passions. Boys are three times more likely than girls to have Asperger's Syndrome.

*Pervasive Developmental Disorder Not Otherwise Specified (PDD-NOS) – This is a catch-all category for people who have some autistic behaviors but don't fit in some categories. These teens have better language skills than classic autism but poorer language skills than Asperger's. They have fewer repetitive behaviors.

Chapter 2 – Comorbid Conditions

A *comorbid condition* is one or more conditions present in addition to the primary diagnosis; in this case, autism,

Emotional, attention, physical and thought disorders are sometimes found in teens with autism. Diagnosis of the comorbid condition is essential to suit the individual needs of the teen. The following are comorbid conditions associated with autism:

*Anxiety- Social Anxiety Disorder (SAD). According to a study published June 25, 2012 in the 'Annals of General Psychiatry,' 29% of teens with autism also have SAD. Higher levels of anxiety were more prevalent in teens with higher IQ's.

*Attention Deficit Hyperactivity Disorder (ADHD)- Previously not listed as a comorbid condition, the DSM-5 now recognizes ADHD as a comorbid condition affecting 28% of teens with autism. Symptoms of ADHD are inattentiveness, hyperactivity, and impulsivity.

*Depression- 'The Annals of General Psychiatry' in the above mentioned study found that 70% of teens with autism have at least one major depressive episode. Chronic unhappiness and loneliness was found in 17% of teens with autism. Some signs to watch for are; fatigue and decreased energy,

pessimistic attitude, loss of interest in hobbies or activities, over-eating or loss of appetite, and trouble sleeping.

*Oppositional Defiant Disorder (ODD) is found in 28% of teens with autism. The Mayo Clinic lists symptoms of ODD as *persistent* arguing, negativity, defiance, and hostility. A teen with ODD may be easily annoyed and become angry and disruptive.

*Gastrointestinal Disorder- There is much debate about a condition often called 'leaky gut.' According to a Harvard study people with ASD frequently have pain or discomfort caused by inflammation of the GI tract. 'Autism Help' states that up to 50% of people with ASD have mild to moderate inflammation. Dr. Andrew Wakefield named the disorder 'autistic enter colitis.' Many medical experts question its existence. While there is still much debate on this subject, in my teaching experience I taught many students with autism who also had intestinal problems.

*Epilepsy- An article in 'Autism Speaks' dated 8/11 states that 1% of the general population has epilepsy compared to 20-40% of people with autism. Epilepsy is more prevalent in the lower-functioning person with autism. Children who have epilepsy have a 5% chance of being diagnosed with autism.

*Intellectual Disability- Researching intellectual disability I found a range of from 25-70% of people with autism have an intellectual disability. Perhaps this wide range is caused by the difficulty in properly assessing a person with autism. I remember attempting to assess a young girl with autism who later went on to win spelling bees and graduate college. She paced around the room and library with me following her asking questions. She giggled as she knowingly gave me incorrect answers.

*Obsessive Compulsive Disorder (OCD)- Obsessive and ritualistic behavior is considered part of ASD. In a study by Dr. Alisa Russell of Bath University published by the 'National Autistic Society', Dr. Russell writes of the difficulty in separating ASD and OCD. The rituals of autism tend to fade some in adolescents. Therefore, if a teen's rituals and intrusive thoughts become more troubling it would be identified as OCD.

*Coordination Disorder- According to 'My Asperger's Child' and 'National Autistic Society' teens with ASD have greater challenges with motor coordination. Also called *dyspraxia* both fine and gross motor skills are affected, resulting in an awkward, unusual gait when running; difficulty riding a bicycle; throwing and catching a ball; tying shoelaces; and pencil grip and writing.

Being a teenager is a stressful time for most teens. Imagine how stressful it must be for a teen with autism, with all these added challenges. The switch from a mostly self-contained classroom environment to a roving schedule adds another layer of stress to a teen who has a need for routine. Until the teen becomes familiar and comfortable with this new routine, s/he may experience added anxiety, even meltdowns.

There are new social, emotional, behavioral and academic demands in high school. While their peers are becoming more independent and sophisticated; starting to prize their social life and even to begin dating; your teen with ASD may not have friends to offer emotional and practical support. The combination of autism, hormones, puberty and high school leaves many parents with mixed emotions- wanting to ensure their child transitions into adult life with the needed strategies, yet at a loss regarding how to accomplish this goal.

The 'Archives of Pediatrics and Adolescents Medicine' noted that 46% of students with ASD experience bullying compared with 11% of the general population. To create a more positive learning environment we must enlist the general education teachers as well as the special education teachers to protect our children. Sometimes a teen with ASD may not even realize that they are being teased and bullied because they have difficulty with social cues. I found one of the most effective ways of stopping bullying was to enlist some general education students to volunteer to be 'friends' with the students with autism. What starts as an assigned act of kindness may turn into a genuine understanding and friendship. And, the friends of the general education student will take notice.

Adults involved with your teen need to assess her/his needs and make a plan to help meet the new demands of high school. Parents, school personnel and specialists must work together to create a clear plan of expectations and goals. Having everyone on board with clear expectations better ensures that your teen will meet the goals.

Part of a High School IEP is an ITP (Individualized Transition Plan). According to special education law (IDEA) an ITP must be in place by your child's 16th birthday, and may be in place as early as her/his 13th birthday. The ITP states that the school district is responsible for preparing your teen for her/his future, including education, employment, and independent living. The ITP is student centered and allows your teen input, some control and choices to the extent that s/he is capable.

The team must decide between a Diploma Track and a Certificate of Completion Track.

The Diploma Track will require your teen to meet educational requirements for a high school diploma.

A high school diploma is necessary if your child will continue in higher education or the military. If completing the Diploma Track your teen's special education services will end at graduation, usually at age 17 or 18. The diploma is sometimes referred to as an *exit document*.

The Certificate of Completion requires your teen to complete one of the following:

-a prescribed alternative course of study

-meet the goals of the IEP

-participate in high school and meet the objectives of a transitional service.

If your teen is working toward the Certificate of Completion s/he may stay in high school through age 22.

It is important to remember that a person's educational rights pass to that person at age 18. However, many 18 year olds with autism are not developmentally ready to make decisions regarding their education; e.g.; they may decide to drop out of school. Prior to your child's 18th birthday discuss the need to be involved with your child's education. Parents may provide a written document signed by the student allowing them to share in any decisions about their child.

The structure of High School poses many challenges for students with autism. Preparing them beforehand so they can anticipate and understand schedules, expectations, and activities will improve the student's adaptation.

An IEP (Individualized Education Program) is a written document developed for each child who is eligible for special education. It is reviewed and revised at least once a year. IEP's contain important information about your child's educational program.

An ITP (Individualized Transition Plan) is a written document that must be in place by your child's 16th birthday, and may be in place as early as their 13th birthday.

The IEP and ITP are developed by a team. The team will include yourself, a general education teacher, a special education teacher, an individual who can interpret test data, an individual representing the district who can commit to providing resources, and people that either you or the district have invited that may include specialists, family, and advocates.

While most of my experience is with IEP's involving elementary children, I have been involved in Jr. High and High School IEP meetings. I noted two differences: 1. The student may have five or more teachers, yet sometimes only one teacher was present. 2. The teachers sometimes had the attitude that *their* classroom rules trumped the IEP accommodations. The higher functioning the student, the less willing the teachers were to make exceptions (in my experience).

If your teen has five teachers and only one shows up for the meeting, you are trusting that his case carrier will relay the information to the other teachers, and that the other teachers will take the time to read and understand the document. A High School teacher may have five classes of 35 students (175 students!) S/he is over-worked and under- paid. Nevertheless, your concern is your child and you need to make that clear. Request that **all** teachers and specialists involved with your child be present.

Once you have all present for the IEP and ITP meeting, be observant of the different teachers' expectations and rules. Make it understood that an IEP is a legal document and not open for interpretation. Take the time to explain your child's strengths and weaknesses. Approach the meeting with the attitude of, "How are you going to help my child?" Once you are known to the school personnel as an involved parent who can be a 'squeaky wheel' if necessary, the school personnel will be more accommodating.

The IEP will list what services your teen receives. By high school these services should already be in place and may include; Language and Speech, Occupational Therapy, Adaptive P.E., counseling, and a one-on-one para professional assigned to your child.

Probably the most important section in a High School IEP is the Accommodations and Modifications section. This is where you **must** make it clear what your teen needs to be successful in class. If it is written in the IEP a teacher cannot legally disregard it.

Accommodations are adaptations (changes) to help students learn the same curriculum as their peers. Some examples are:

-audio books

-using a keyboard for written assignments

-preferential seating (sitting close to the teacher, having the same seat in each classroom, etc.)

-extra time

-large print

-visual aids

-teaching through a multi-sensory approach (visual, auditory, kinesthetic)

-shorter assignments

-reduction of homework

-main ideas highlighted in textbooks

-teacher prompts student to turn in homework

-transitions between classes five minutes early

-peer buddy

-teacher must notify you if your child is missing an assignment and give a week to turn in the missing assignment (This accommodation is highly recommended for all!)

Modifications generally refer to a change in either what is being taught or what is expected from the student. These are appropriate for a student pursuing a certificate of completion rather than a high school diploma. Some examples of modifications are:

-specialized curriculum

-lower performance goals

-use of a calculator for math

-fewer spelling words

-adjusted grading

-tests read to student

-slower-paced instruction

A good transition plan (ITP) can change your teen's future. The ITP addresses preparing your teen for their future adult life. Many parents are surprised to discover that once their child leaves the public school system there is no guarantee of adult services.

An ITP should include academic, vocational, and independent living skills as well as social skills and community experiences.   If you are not involved with your local Regional Center, become involved while your child is still in school. Ask your school for a list of agencies that serve adults.

By now you have probably attended many IEP meetings and received a copy of your parent rights at each one. Parent Rights vary little from state to state. In California a parent has the right:

*to participate in any decision regarding your child's educational placement. You should be included in the decision-making process. The psychologist shouldn't walk into the meeting with her/his mind already made up as to what FAPE (free appropriate public education) will be offered.

*to refer your child for testing. By high school I assume your child has already been assessed, diagnosed, and is receiving services. If this isn't the case, your child most likely is a very high-functioning child. To get your child assessed, go to the district's special services office and put in a written request for testing. Don't take 'no' for an answer.

*to be included in the development of the IEP and ITP. You are part of the team. No decisions should be made without your input. Come prepared with an idea of what is acceptable to you. You may want to bring an advocate or friend. Don't be afraid to say, "This isn't acceptable." Or "This meeting is over. We will meet again after I speak with an advocate."

*to written notice of any change in your child's educational program.

*to an independent educational assessment. If you disagree with the school psychologist's assessment, you have the right to another assessment administered by an impartial party. (I have *rarely* seen an initial diagnosis of autism made by a school psychologist. I can only recall it happening once in 35 years of teaching. With high-functioning autism and Asperger's Syndrome you will probably need to have assessments by a third party. I have seen a school psychologist tell a parent their child doesn't have autism, when the child had been previously diagnosed. The parent insisted on a third party assessment and, of course, the child did indeed still have autism.)

*to have your child 'stay put.' If there is a disagreement in the meeting; e.g.; the school wants to move your child to another class and you disagree, you have the right for your child to stay in her/his current setting until the disagreement is resolved.

*to a hearing regarding any disagreement between you and the school district regarding your child's FAPE.

You've created the best school environment for your teen. You have a thick folder containing IEP's, ITP's, resources, teacher information, test data. It's not easy being your teen's advocate, but you're doing it.

Now let's talk about some ways to help your teen at home.

There's no question that teens with autism enter their teen years with a disadvantage. The rules of society are changing for them, and people with autism are all about the 'rules.' They crave routine and knowing what to expect. They may retreat into themselves, experiencing loneliness and confusion. Because of autism your teen may not communicate how s/he is feeling. Where non-autistic youth withdraw from parents to hang out with their friends, your teen may have no friends. Your teen may not feel safe, may even feel threatened by all the changes in her/his life. Some will regress into childhood interests, trying to recapture a simpler time.

How do you help? The autism spectrum is so large there is not a 'one size fits all' solution, but here are some ideas that may help your teen feel more secure and in control of her/his life.

*Social Stories- Remember the stories you used when your child was younger? They can still help. Write or tell about a teenager beginning high school and how s/he handles some of the challenges. Be specific to what is happening right now with your teen.

*Visual Supports- A visual schedule or calendar comforts teens with autism. They **see** what their day entails and know what to expect.

*Role- playing- Your young child loved it and so will your teen. Make a game out of it and have fun. Praise when skills practiced in role-playing are carried over into real-life experiences.

*Teach Self-Management Skills- As a young child your teen may have expressed her/his frustration with meltdowns. As a teen this is unacceptable. Teach ways to handle frustration, e.g., deep breathing, counting, walking away, a practice line to say to bullies ("Leave me alone!"). When I taught social skills some of the most empowering lessons were on self-discipline. I remember one boy who responded to frustration by yelling. I could see his 'aha' moment when he realized he could control his actions. He embraced self-discipline; after one lesson on using kind words he told me, "I'm going to teach this to my mom!"

*Create Social Opportunities- Create opportunities to practice the new skills. This will boost your teen's self-esteem.

*Allow down time after school- Give your teen some time to relax and unwind after school. Don't start homework right after school.

*Give choices- Let her/him have power over some life choices.

*Let her/him choose their own clothes- This is tough, but if your daughter wants to wear her leopard print PJ bottoms to school, let her.

*Watch for anxiety and depression- As mentioned in chapter 2, many teens with autism also experience depression and anxiety. If you see signs of anxiety or depression seek professional help.

*Be patient

*Be kind

Positives!

There are so many positives teens on the autism spectrum possess. While parents of other teens are waiting for their child to come home on a Saturday night, you know where your child is. Teens on the spectrum:

-have no interest in pop culture

-have their own fashion style, rarely caring if their shoes are a name-brand

-rarely lie

-live in the moment

-are still your friend

-don't judge others

-have amazing memories

-are usually not interested in driving

-are kind and innocent

-are sometimes gifted

Some famous people with autism:

*Temple Grandin

*Susan Boyle

*Albert Einstein

*Darryl Hannah

*Dan Aykroyd

As Temple Grandin said, "We are different, not less."

Conclusion

I sincerely hope that this book has been helpful and informative to parents, teachers, and all those that love someone with autism. With the right strategies and teamwork, your teen will have the best life possible. Though at times your journey may be difficult, always be patient and kind.

Please take a few minutes to give this book a review on Amazon and visit me on Facebook @ Cindy Stringer Wismer Author and Author Central on Amazon.

Sources

Annals of General Psychiatry

National Autistic Society

Autism Speaks

Harvard University

Autism Help

Mayo Clinic

My Asperger Child

The Autism Society of Los Angeles

Archives of Pediatrics and Adolescent Medicine

WebMD

Psychology Today

Other Books by Cindy Stringer Wismer

Never Push and Never Pull

A Guide for Parents and Teachers of Children with Special Needs, including Autism

Stars in the Sand

The Magic Sands

ADHD in Children- ranked #1 on Amazon in special education 6/9/14

ADHD in Adults

Autism in Toddlers

Autism in Children